DISS AND DISTRICT

A Portrait in Old Picture Postcards

by

Dennis Cross

S. B. Publications
1991

CONTENTS

CONTENTS CONTINUED

Abbreviations used: c. – circa; p.u. – postally used.

INTRODUCTION

Diss is situated in South Norfolk on the Norfolk-Suffolk border, twenty miles from Norwich, twenty-two miles from Ipswich and thirty miles from the coast.

South Norfolk is an area of unspoilt charm, with picturesque villages scattered in the rolling countryside and attractive towns providing a wealth of history. Some people might now find it hard to believe, but South Norfolk was once one of the most densely populated parts of Britain. That was around the time of the Norman Conquest, but even before the Normans other invaders helped to shape the area. The Romans came, and they were followed by immigrants from Germany and Denmark, who founded new settlements and cleared the forests.

Farming was the foundation of the area's wealth and helped build the prosperity of towns like Diss. Diss is mentioned in the Domesday Book as a moderately sized Royal Manor of no great importance, but when a market was established it brought wealth to the town. Flemish weavers came from across the Channel and for many centuries wool and linen were the chief industries. These continued to flourish throughout the 16th and 17th centuries and many of the town's historic buildings from that era remain intact; for example the Dolphin in the Market Place and Fair Green houses.

A focal point of the town through the years has been the Mere and, in fact, Diss gets its name from 'Dic' or 'Disce' which is Saxon for 'ditch of standing water'. When a serious fire broke out in Mere Street in 1640, it was only the water from the lake, which covers 5½ acres, that saved the houses in the street. The greatest event of all came more than 250 years later in 1891, when the Mere completely froze over. The highlight was a canival on ice when hundreds of skaters donned fancy dress to dance to the strains of a 30-strong band playing in the middle of the ice.

Denmark Green in Diss may be quiet and tranquil today but it has a colourful and lively past. Known as Cock Street Green until 1863, it was a hive of activity for nearly 700 years when the Cock Street Fair took place in late October and early November. It was a market for local produce, but is perhaps more famous for being the scene of the barbaric pastimes of bull and bear baiting and cock fighting.

The postcards in this book depicting Diss and the villages of the surrounding parishes of Scole, Burston, Bressingham. Gissing, Shimpling, Dickleburgh, Wortham, Mellis and Palgrave, each have their own unique topography and history. The great attraction of these picture postcards produced by local photographers such as G.S. Pearse, A.D. Maling and W. Nunn is that they illustrate so vividly a way of life and scenes that are so different from our own, yet still within living memory. I trust that this book will go some way in preserving for posterity the not too distant past.

Dennis Cross,
Diss,
March 1991

THE RAILWAY BRIDGE, c. 1909

In 1848 Messrs. Ransomes of Ipswich erected an iron bridge across the road leading into Diss ready to take one of Norfolk's first railways to London which opened in late 1849. The bridge is decorated for the Royal Norfolk Show of 1909, which was held on meadows near Walcot Green.

CHURCH STREET, p.u. 1908

This view is looking west towards the Market Place. Church Street was formerly called Dirt Street. By this street, in what is now the churchyard, was the 15th-century Guildhall, later used as a Grammar School and sold in 1846 for £80 and then demolished. Number 17, the house with the lady near the window, was scheduled as being of historical interest, but it was demolished to make room for the Diss Library in the 1960s.

Church Street, Diss

CHURCH STREET, c. 1930

Church Street looking east. This view shows a road branching to the right which used to be called Rector's Entry; the entry to the Old Rectory adjoining Victoria Road. On the left of this road was a garden nursery and meadows. Today this is where Uplands Way now starts, and then Clare House, named after the poet, John Clare.

THE CHURCH HALL, p.u. 1912

The Church Hall was situated at the junction of Mere Street with Park Road. The Hall was erected in 1898 by Stroud Lincoln Cocks, Esq. of The Uplands, Diss, at a cost of £1,000 and used for meetings connected with church work. It also served as a parochial lending library until it was demolished in the 1970s to make way for modern development.

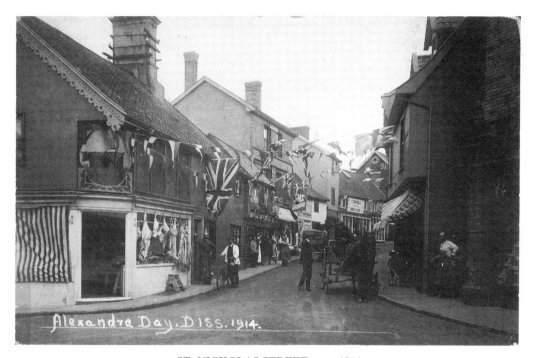

Alexandra Day. DISS. 1914.

ST. NICHOLAS STREET, p.u. 1914

St. Nicholas Street, looking west from St. Mary's Church, decorated for Alexandra Rose Day which still exists and was founded in honour of Queen Alexandra, with the proceeds going to childrens' charities and held originally on Queen Victoria's birthday in May. The butcher's shop with meat hanging in front of the window belonged to a Walter Anness; this shop is still in existence as a butcher's shop today.

HALL HILLS HOUSE, c. 1910

Hall Hills House stood on the site of a house which was a 14-acre sheep farm until 1870, when it was sold to the Taylor family and demolished to build a Victorian residence shown in this picture. In the mid 1870s it was occupied by the Downton family until the early 1930s. This house lasted nearly one hundred years before being demolished to make way for a modern housing estate named Hall Hills.

THE COURT, c. 1909

This building was situated at the bottom of Vinces Lane, which is now an industrial site. It was first called "The Court", the owner being a William Betts. It was opened in 1907 as a Roman Catholic Girls' Boarding and Day School, and was owned by a Reg Chase, a miller. The priest in charge at the school was the Rev. G. Bompass. After the second world war, the school was disbanded and the house was bought by a local farmer and again called "The Court", until it was finally demolished in the 1960s.

J. ALDRICH, MARKET HILL, c. 1903

John Aldrich's shop, established in 1832, was situated just off the Market Place and at the start of Market Hill. The shop was decorated to celebrate the Coronation of Edward VII in 1903. A disastrous fire on 17th June, 1938, resulted in the shop being gutted even though it was attended by 5 fire engines and plenty of water from the Mere at the rear of the property. Larter & Ford's now occupy this site.

PARK AND UNITARIAN CHAPEL, p.u. 1913

This chapel was erected in 1822 as a Unitarian Chapel seating 300 people. Today it is used by the Montgomerie Lodge of Freemasons, and is called Masonic Hall. The meadow in the picture is now a park for recreation. The cows provide a peaceful scene.

BUILDING THE WATER TOWER
AT DISS. 1912.

THE WATER TOWER, 1912

The Diss water tower and works cost £8,000, with building work commencing in January, 1912. Mains construction and pipe laying followed shortly afterwards (see page 50). By 1922 approximately 12 million gallons a year were supplied to the town. By 1962, the water supply had risen to 90 million gallons a year, after a new bore and tower had been constructed; the latter dedicated to the Jubilee.

AUCTION DAY, p.u. 1913

Auction day for sheep in Diss. This scene shows a special sale of rams, ewes and lambs – these were normally held in August with sales for lambs only held in June. At these sales between 15,000 and 20,000 sheep were sold, having been driven from various farms in the district. In the late afternoon special trains were ordered from the Great Eastern Railway to transport the sheep to various destinations. This view is taken looking east towards Shelfanger Road from the sale ground on Roydon Road. These sales ceased several years ago and now no livestock is sold in Diss by auction.

MERE STREET, c. 1910

Looking south along Mere Street and showing The Ship public house and the Waveney Tea Rooms. Mr. Frederick Cook is seen in this picture with his horse-drawn funeral hearse together with his staff and horse-drawn carriages. In addition to being a funeral furnisher he also ran a public house, a posting establishment and livery and bait stables. From the first floor windows there was a fine view looking out across the Mere. Sadly these buildings were taken down in 1968 and a supermarket built in its place; this has now been replaced by two shops.

MERE STREET, c. 1935

Mere Street runs from the Market Place to Victoria Road. The majority of the 18th-century houses have nearly all been turned into shops. The Leicester Building Society at No. 1, Mere Street is partly Tudor with a carved herald angel on its 15th-century timber frame, and was originally the house of a guild priest. The Sun Inn has some particularly good interior features and a good view across the Mere. This picture, looking north up Mere Street, shows petrol pumps, a garage and buildings belonging then to W.D. Chitty; the site is now occupied by a supermarket. The front gardens on the right-hand side have gone also.

THE MARKET PLACE, p.u. 1910

The Market Place still holds a weekly market on Fridays when stalls cover the area. On the left-hand side of the road, the post office, which opened in 1953, stands on the site of The Bell public house. Further down the street, the Co-op was built on the site of an old house called 'The Terrace'. On the opposite side of the road The Kings Head and The Star public houses have both been demolished and modern shops built in their place.

THE CO-OP, MERE STREET, c. 1915

This picture shows the first bakery and shop owned by the Co-op, situated in Mere Street, before moving to a larger shop in Victoria Road. Most people remember this being a tea shop. Currys then occupied this shop over a very long period and only recently moved out. It is now occupied by The Trading Post, selling everyday needs.

PARK ROAD, c. 1912

Looking west along Park Road and photographed at the junction of Mere Street and Victoria Road. On the right is the Chapel, belonging to the Free Methodists, which also had a large school room at the back where the Good Templars and Band of Hope held their meetings. These buildings and the two houses further along the road have all been demolished to make way for a garage and a supermarket. On the left were meadows stretching down to the River Waveney; the land now occupied by factories, a bus station and a car park.

PARK ROAD, c. 1910

Facing east along Park Road at the junctions with Denmark Street, Fair Green and Croft Lane. This was a private road with footpath status with gates at each end until around 1910 when it was made a public highway with easier access to Victoria Road. On the right of this picture, note the small building attached to the Denmark Arms public house, photographed just before being demolished. At a later date, the house and buildings on the opposite side of the road were also demolished to allow an improved access to Denmark Street.

ST. NICHOLAS STREET, p.u. 1911

St. Nicholas Street, formerly Half Moon Street, derived its name from The Half Moon Inn which stood on the site of Cobb's Cycle Shop. Halfway down, where it divides from Market Hill, is The Greyhound Inn formerly The Pilgrims Inn. King James I is alleged to have stayed there. This picture shows a Church Procession passing the Corn Hall for a rally on the Grammar School field.

ST. NICHOLAS STREET, c. 1890

This shop was situated at the top of Market Hill where the road joins St. Nicholas Street; the building is now occupied by a restaurant. In the Middle Ages, the site was originally St. Nicholas Chapel. According to records there used to be a tunnel running from the Greyhound to this chapel, and a graveyard existed where Gaze's offices now stand on Market Hill.

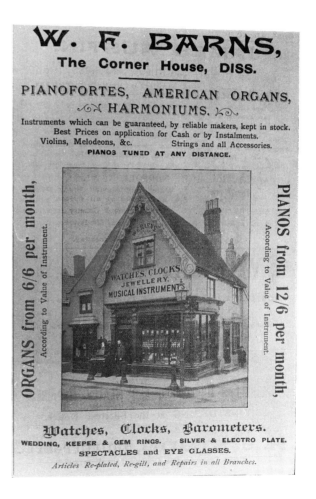

W. F. BARNS,
The Corner House, DISS.

PIANOFORTES, AMERICAN ORGANS,
HARMONIUMS,

Instruments which can be guaranteed, by reliable makers, kept in stock.
Best Prices on application for Cash or by Instalments.
Violins, Melodeons, &c.   Strings and all Accessories.
PIANOS TUNED AT ANY DISTANCE.

ORGANS from 6/6 per month,
According to Value of Instrument.

PIANOS from 12/6 per month,
According to Value of Instrument.

WATCHES, CLOCKS,
JEWELLERY,
MUSICAL INSTRUMENTS

Watches, Clocks, Barometers.
WEDDING, KEEPER & GEM RINGS.   SILVER & ELECTRO PLATE.
SPECTACLES and EYE GLASSES.
Articles Re-plated, Re-gilt, and Repairs in all Branches.

THE BOARD SCHOOL, p.u. 1909

The Board Shool was situated off Victoria Road behind Mavery House. It was erected in 1860, enlarged in 1874 and 1895 to accommodate 480 children. Thomas M. Pullen was the headmaster in 1900. This school has now closed and is awaiting the developer. In 1911 the population of Diss totalled 3,769.

THE BOARD SCHOOL, 1928–29

In the 1920s the Board School was renamed the Council School. The headmaster was Mr. J. Cushing. Miss I.D. Brown was the girls' mistress. The class names in photograph are as follows: *Top row (Left to right):* H. Smith, E. Neve, H. Cullum, W. Harold, W. Foster & S. Rice. *Middle row:* C. Sutton, F. Loynes, A. Farrow, E. Pitchers, H. Hines and G. Bloomfield. *Bottom row:* F. Hume, T. Bloomfield, H. George, V. Bendell, Barham and H. Mortimer.

The Diss Soda Water Works. Gostling & Co., Proprietors.

SODA WATER WORKS, c. 1894

Gostling Soda Water Works was situated at the east end of Church Street adjoining what was then Finchams Meadows, later to become Anness's Meadows and later Uplands Way. Gostling's used to manufacture soda water priced at 2s6d (12½p) per dozen bottles, also lemonade, ginger beer, gingerade, seltzer water and various other drinks. All the water used in the manufacture of drinks came from a deep well in Finchams Meadows. In the 1890s horse-drawn wagons distributed to the local public houses and chemists as shown in this picture. After the first world war, Doubleday took over this business and then enlarged their factory in Denmark Street. St. Mary's Court now stands on this site.

GOSTLING & COMPANY, CHEMIST, c. 1900

Gostling & Co., chemist was situated at the junction of Denmark and Crown Streets (now St. Nicholas Street); one of two shops they owned in Diss. Today Lloyds Bank stands on this site. In 1900, they dispensed, manufactured and sold many products including: pepsine wine at 2/- (10p) a bottle, cod liver oil emulsion, anti-catarrh salts, carbolic soap, butter powder and many other household items.

BUTTONS MILL
DISS

BUTTONS MILL, c. 1890

Diss used to have ten windmills. One was at Holly Farm at the Heywood, two were just inside the parish of Roydon, and one in Shelfanger Road beyond the brush factory. Another stood at the bottom of Chapel Street where there is now a car park, and one in Croft Lane near the junction with Roydon Road. If you had crossed Diss Common in the last century you would have seen no less than five windmills. There were also two mills in Rose Lane; one at the corner of Stuston Road and one in a field off Sandy Lane. There is only one remaining; Buttons Mill which is now a residence owned by Mr. Robert Manning. This is best viewed from the railway line when travelling by train towards Ipswich.

POLICE STATION, p.u. 1909

Diss Police Station was built and opened in 1905 in Roydon Road. In 1962 a new and larger station building was opened in Stanley Road. Charles James was the inspector with two constables under him. Previously, the police headquarters was at Pulham Market, but there was a prison cell for offenders at the Dolphin public house which is now converted into a small shop "The Keyhole Antiques".

4th NORFOLKS, MERE STREET, p.u. 1914

This view was taken at the junction of Mere Street with Victoria and Park Roads showing young men leaving Diss to join the 4th Norfolks for service in the first world war, marching to Diss Station to travel to Norwich. The Church Hall is on the left and the Methodist Church is on the right. Notice the gas lamp in the left foreground – all the town was lit by gas in those days.

THE WESLEYAN CHURCH, c. 1911

The Wesleyan Church was first erected in 1819 along with a school and then rebuilt in 1833. This has also been demolished and the site is now occupied by Mavery House. The present Church opened in 1964, built on land adjoining The Causeway between Chapel Street and Victoria Road.

We went to
Sunday School here.

THE MERE, p.u. 1907

This view shows the Mere frozen over in 1907 when it became a skater's paradise. The biggest freeze-ups were in 1827 and 1891, the latter lasting for thirteen weeks, when a grand carnival and fancy dress fête, with Diss Town Band, were held. Skaters came from Ipswich, Woodbridge, Stowmarket, Saxmundham and Harleston by rail and road. In total no fewer than 5,000 people took part or were spectators. Hundreds were in fancy-dress costumes and the ice by this time was seven inches thick. Every few years since then the Mere has frozen for a short time with big freeze-ups in 1939–40, 1947 and in 1963 when a big party was held again. Notice the hospital standing in the background.

MERE STREET, p.u. 1909

Mere Street shown decorated for the Royal Norfolk Show which is normally held in mid-June. This view is looking south towards Victoria Road. Most shops on the right-hand side have changed completely. The Royal Norfolk Show was held at Walcot every few years on meadows around Walcot Hall, the last being on 15th and 16th June, 1939. The admission price was 3/- (15p) for the first day, and 2/- (10p) for the second day. For Diss people this event meant a day off work or school, visitors arriving by train as very few people owned cars in those days.

MANOR GARDENS, c. 1905

Manor Gardens provided the venue for this Church Garden Fête. The Gardens were situated opposite the brewery, between Shelfanger Road and a footpath off Mount Street and owned by the Manor House. What fine hats the ladies are wearing! In the late 1930s part of the gardens were sold off and replaced by new houses and, adjoining Shelfanger Road, a sale ground for poultry and garden produce by Thos. Wm. Gaze & Sons. This was closed in the late 1970s and new houses built on the site.

CHARABANC TRIP, 1914

Ernest Froud with his charabanc about to set off for a trip to the coast with members of the Wesleyan Methodist Chapel. This was one of the first charabancs to be owned and operated from Diss. The top speed was about 15 m.p.h. and the wooden-spoked wheels with solid tyres must have provided a very uncomfortable journey!

Victoria Rd DISS.

Maling Ph.

VICTORIA ROAD, c. 1910

Victoria Road, formerly called Diss Common, ran from the Church Hall to Frenze river bridge. The renaming was decided by the Board of Health – predecessors of the D.U.C.C. – at a meeting in 1863 when the Authorities wanted to mark the occasion of the betrothal of Prince Edward (later Edward VII) to Princess Alexandra of Denmark in 1862. This scene shows Diss Co-op in its new premises and Watson & Smith's Garage which was knocked down in the early 1960s to make way for a modern garage (now Gales). Further down, the road has changed beyond all recognition.

VICTORIA ROAD, c. 1905

This picture was taken at the junction of Station and Victoria Roads. On the right the site is now Jewson's builders' merchants. Victoria Road used to be a rough dirt track across what was called Diss Common or Moor. This commenced where Gales' Garage now stands to the Frenze river bridge. Triangular in shape and extending over 90 acres, the Common was a mile long and 600 yards across at its widest point. Copyhold tenants had right of commonage for great beasts, but sheep grazing was forbidden. In 1693 a John Cracknell was charged with having put seventeen sheep on the common (originally called Diss Moor). He was fined 2s.6d (12½p) for trespass and damage done.

Cromer Express (60 miles an hour) passing through Diss.

DISS RAILWAY STATION, c. 1911

The Eastern Union Railway came to Diss on 2nd July, 1849 – a service of four trains in each direction, weekdays only, from London to Burston. The route beyond Burston to Norwich, giving a much shorter London route than the rival Eastern Counties line, came into operation five months later on 12th December, 1849. A journey time of five hours from start to destination, stopping at all stations. Most expresses started from Cromer around 1900 and did not stop until they arrived at Ipswich.

Victoria Road, Diss. J 3903. *(Randall's Series).*

shop was where I used to go to get grandad Keats cigarettes.

VICTORIA ROAD, c. 1930

Looking towards Diss and showing the sub post office on the right; the postmistress at the time was a Miss Kate E. Randall. Victoria Road, once part of Diss Common, was the site of the execution of Robert Carleton on 5th April, 1742 – the last public execution in the area. Carleton, a Diss tailor, had an assistant, Lincoln, who was in love with a Mary Frost. Carleton, afraid of losing Lincoln's services, forbode their marriage. One evening he invited Mary to his home for dinner which consisted of boiled mutton accompanied with salt laced with a deadly poison. Mary died an agonising death shortly afterwards. Carleton was arrested, tried at Thetford Assizes and sentenced to be hanged in chains on Diss Common. 5,000 people watched the grim spectacle.

PUMP HILL, c. 1905

Locals still call Pump Hill instead of Market Hill as there used to be a pump near Barclays Bank. Another pump could be found in Mount Street just past the Rectory. All the buildings on the right of this picture were owned by the Bobby family; notice their advertisements on the walls and blinds. Only the building shown centre right has disappeared to make way for the Trustee Savings Bank.

VIEW FROM THE CHURCH TOWER, p.u. 1912

The town of Diss stands principally on an acclivity overlooking a mere. The Mere extends over six acres, supplied a natural spring, and averages about 20 feet in depth. For many years it had the reputation locally of being bottomless. The Waveney was once a much wider expanse of water, and probably this lake is a remnant. The Mere receives most of the surplus rain water from the town and when full it discharges itself into the River Waveney via an overflow pipe. It was stocked with fish in 1904, abounds with eels, and is said to contain rare fish called "chasers" (china carp).

BAPTIST CHAPEL, DENMARK STREET, c. 1912

The Baptist Chapel was erected in 1860 costing £2,100 and seated 650 people. It replaced an older chapel in Croft Lane adjoining the junction with Croft Close. Notice the cottage on the far side of the chapel – now demolished and a school room built in its place.

MOUNT STREET, p.u. 1910

This winter scene shows The Cedars and The Manor House; The Cedars is situated on the right-hand side of Mount Street facing the Parish Fields. For many years doctors practiced here, though during the 19th century part of the building was used as a school for young ladies.

MARKET PLACE, c. 1918

Peace Celebrations taking place on 19th July, 1919, in the Market Place in front of The Bell public house and Nice's cycle shop. Notice the wide variety of hats.

FINCHAM'S MEADOWS, c. 1904

Fincham's Meadows later became Anness's Meadows; this view has now changed beyond recognition. In the early 1950s the Secondary Modern Schools were built on this site, later to become the High School. The trees on the left-hand side of this picture border Walcot Road.

Church Tower. Diss.   Nº 25.

THE CHURCH OF ST. MARY THE VIRGIN, p.u. 1909

The Church, dedicated to St. Mary the Virgin, is a large building of flint and free-stone with panelled buttresses, mostly in late Decorated and Perpendicular styles of architecture. The church consists of a chancel, cleresteried nave with aisles, north and south porches and a fine square embattled tower at its west end, erected in 1791, containing a clock with eight bells.

DISS HOSPITAL, c. 1905

Diss Hospital was formerly a young ladies' school which was opened in 1862. The building, overlooking the Mere, was erected in 1895 and called Grassmere House. It became a hospital at the turn of the century, opened by Mrs. Francis Taylor with Dr. Speirs as Medical Superintendent. The electricity supply came from the brewery along Shelfanger Road. It later became the Headquarters of the British Legion but later demolished in the early 1960s to make way for the new Conservative Club named "Grassmere".

DISS HOSPITAL

DISS MARATHON, 13th March, 1909

Marathon races in Diss were run annually. They normally started from The Crown public house then following a 14-mile course around the surrounding villages ending back at The Crown. Runners took part from all over Norfolk and Suffolk, the winner being presented with a cup.

THE CROWN HOTEL, c. 1916

The Crown and Commercial Hotel, a large prestigious building, was built in 1878. Ernest Slade was the proprietor in 1916. At the rear of the building, there were stables for his horses and a garage for carriages which were used for conveying customers to and from the railway station. The bowling green (shown top right) was situated at the rear of The Cherry Tree public house. The stables and buildings have now been sold, parts of the hotel have been leased and the Crown interior has been reduced in size and is just a public house today.

MERE STREET, c. 1930

Mere Street contains many 18th-century houses which have now been turned into shops. The prominent building on the right-hand side is probably The King's Head, a 17th-century coaching inn, now divided into shops. The houses on the left have all been converted into shops.

DENMARK GREEN, p.u. 1916

Denmark Green used to be known as Fair Green after the November Fair, first granted by Henry II. It has also been called Cock Street Green after the cruel sport of cock fighting which occurred here until the 19th century; Diss Cock Street Fair was abolished by the then Home Secretary in 1872. This view was taken looking towards Denmark Bridge, and shows the Post Office, now a private house, and a row of thatched houses which were demolished in the late 1950s. Modern houses have now been built here.

MOUNT STREET, p.u. 1912

Mount Street was formerly called Mound or Smith Street. This view looking north from the church shows the Post Office which was open on weekdays, 8 a.m. to 8 p.m., and on Sundays 8 a.m. to 10 a.m. Letters were delivered four times a day. The postmaster in 1900 was a William Funnel Pearce. Before the 1900s mail was brought from Scole by mail cart drawn by horses. Railways changed this practice and Diss then became the postal centre for the whole district. This post office closed in 1953, and the building was rebuilt for Social Security Offices. A new post office was opened adjoining the Market Place. Further along the street a group of houses were demolished to make way for a car park and health centre.

First Post Van Diss

EARLY POST VAN, c. 1927

The first motorised vehicles used for postal deliveries in Diss were Model-T Fords, with wooden spoked wheels, no self-starter, hand-operated windscreen wipers and half doors which gave no protection against inclement weather. The only protective clothing issued was a peaked cap. When not in use these vans were kept and serviced in a building at the rear of The Saracen's Head. Identified on the picture are Mr. Copping of Roydon and Mr. W. Nunn, a postman in Diss.

PIPE-LAYING, c. 1912

In 1912 Diss had its first water tower (see page 10) and piped water mains were laid down in most streets shortly afterwards. This scene shows a gang of pipe-layers busy in Mount Street outside the Manor House, the home of the well-known Taylor family who lived here for nearly 200 years.

ARRIVAL OF THE TERRITORIALS, c. 1914

The Territorials marching from Diss railway station, after the arrival of a special troop train, via Victoria Road, Mere Street, Mount Street, Walcot Road and finally to the Camp at Walcot Hall where they were to remain for several weeks to carry out training manœuvres in the area. This photograph was taken at the top of Mount Street.

DISS FOOTBALL TEAM, 1946–47 SEASON

Diss Town Football Club played all their matches at Roydon Road beside the sale yard until the end of the 1984 season. When this photograph was taken they had just played Sheringham in the league, winnng 10–1. Players and supporters are as follows: *Back row (left to right):* C. Edwards, B. Thaxter, P. Nash, C. Piper, T. Long, S. Sharp, R. Cordy, C. Goold. *Middle row:* P. Rook, V. Bloomfield, B. Rice, J. Baldwin, C. Colson. *Front:* E. Cobb.

ROYDON RD. DISS. 5.

ROYDON ROAD, p.u. 1915

Photographed close to the junction with Croft Lane and Roydon Road. The house standing on the right-hand side of this photograph used to be the Lodge for Hall Hills which is now demolished. This scene has changed completely as modern houses have been built on both sides of the road today.

BELL RINGER AND ENTERTAINER, c. 1905

The gentleman in this photograph was a bell ringer and local entertainer. He would travel miles around the district with his donkey and cart to entertain at garden parties and fêtes. He is standing just off Victoria Road near the pedestrian crossing. Behind the trees to the left was the Methodist Church.

DISS TOWN BAND, p.u. 1911

Diss Town Band played at fêtes, garden parties, carnivals, special events and military processions. All members were required to practice at least once a week in a carpenter's workshop in Harrison's Yard, just off Shelfanger Road. The photograph was taken behind The Kings Head yard in Mere Street.

WALCOT HALL, p.u. 1913

Soldiers preparing their bedding at Walcot Hall where they were camping and on training manœuvres. Their camp covered most of the meadows around the Hall and also the playing fields used by the High School.

WALCOT HALL, c. 1900

Walcot Hall is situated north-east of Diss Church and set in over 130 acres of agricultural land and meadows. The Hall itself is surrounded by gardens with a large moat and was owned then by a Charles Chase, Esq. The meadows around the Hall played host to many events including the Royal Norfolk Show, rallies, agricultural shows, and a military camp which was established before and sited there during the first world war. In the 1920s, the Hall was substantially renovated and enlarged. In 1991 it will be further enlarged and turned into a nursing home.

DISS SALVATION ARMY BAND, c. 1914

Diss Salvation Army first held their meetings in an upstairs room at F. Bullock's motor garage in Denmark Street until 1928 when they moved to their present premises in Sunnyside. The old building was purchased by T.G. Gaze and used as a store until demolished for the pig market to be enlarged. This postcard shows the band with all their fine instruments. Their names are as follows: *Back row (left to right):* E. Green (Band Master), H. Kent, W. Easto, A. Leeder. *Middle row:* E. Leeder, T. Green, T. Dye, B. Leader. *Front row:* C. Clark, W. Green, unknown, G.N. Rackham, unknown, A. Flatman.

ROYDON RECTORY DISS.

ROYDON RECTORY, p.u. 1911

Roydon is a parish and village on the border of Norfolk with Suffolk and situated a mile west of Diss. The old rectory stood on the site on what is now Waterloo Avenue. It served as the rectory to St. Remigius Church which is further along the main road. A new rectory was built nearer the main road during the early 1960s.

EARLY FIRE ENGINE, c. 1929

On 17th April, 1929 a new fire engine, known as a Merryweather trailer pump, arrived in Diss to replace the old fire appliance known as 'Niagara' which had served the town for many years. It was towed by Chitty's and West's garage breakdown vehicles to fires and was housed in Will's Yard in Chapel Street. The fire crew were all members of the Rice family: George, Reggie, Bert, Jack, Ernest, Harry (Film) and Stanley. The man on the far left was demonstrating the operation of the fire engine.

MR. FRANK ALGAR, MILKMAN, c. 1925

Mr. Frank Algar owned a dairy farm at Walcot Green. After early morning milking he would commence his daily milk round. This photograph was taken in Shelfanger Road.

BRESSINGHAM FORGE, p.u. 1914

Bressingham Forge stood at the crossroads which is now near the centre of the village. The roads lead to South Lopham, Fersfield, Diss and Roydon. This view looking towards Roydon has changed beyond recognition. The blacksmith, Frederick Smith, is seen here fitting and fixing new shoes to a horse, and a roadman is sitting alongside a heap of stones having his lunch. In 1911 Bressingham had a population of 504.

BURROUGHES MILL, BRESSINGHAM, c. 1900

Bressingham tower mill was situated half-a-mile on the right from the Bressingham Garden House public house. It was a wooden octagonal self-winding mill with four floors and four patent sails driving two pairs of French burr stones and a floor mill. It was originally owned by Mr. Henry Hudson who rented the mill to the miller, Herbert Ernest Burroughes, who paid £36 per annum. When the mill and house were auctioned on 15th February, 1901, Mr. Burroughes bought the mill and buildings. Later the mill was demolished to make way for a modern building, then enlarged to make it the size it is today. This picture shows painters and carpenters who had just finished painting and repairing the mill with a wagon load of corn waiting to be ground into flour.

BURROUGHES MILL BRESSINGHAM

BURSTON RAILWAY STATION, c. 1900

Burston is three miles north by east from Diss. The station was opened by the Eastern Union Railway on 2nd July, 1849 to London, followed by the section to Norwich Victoria on 12th December, 1849; journey times to Norwich taking 46 minutes. Freight trains operated from the station carrying coal and agricultural produce, with two corn and coal merchants, Robinson Brothers and William Smith & Sons, based nearby. At the turn of the century a Mr. George Nathaniel Flude was the master. Many excursions from the station were organised; In 1900 third class travel to Yarmouth cost 2/6d (12½p) return. Sadly this station closed on 5th November, 1966. The buildings, platform and signal box have all been demolished except the old ticket office which is now in private hands.

BURSTON FOOTBALL TEAM, 1932

Burston Football Team photographed after winning the Harleston Charity Cup. The game was played on the field near the junction of Market Lane with the Diss road. The names are as follows: *Back row (left to right):* Jimmy Ling (owner of the pitch), Jack Downing (Secretary), Bert Wilby, Tom Potter, Herby Garnham, Percy Wilby, Gerry Cole, Bert Youngman, Billy Mickleburgh. *Front row:* Tom Lockwood, Bill Piper, Dick Wilby, Cecil Bloomfield, Aubrey Ringer.

BURSTON BOARD SCHOOL, 1905

Burston Board School and the master's house were built in 1875 at a cost of £850. The school was enlarged in 1895 at a further cost of £140 to accommodate 90 children; the average daily attendance only 63. At the time Mr. William Thomas Sutton was headmaster and the population of the village was 314.

BURSTON POST OFFICE, c. 1905

Burston post office and shop were situated near the church facing The Green and The Crown public house. In 1905 the shopkeeper was William Boulton who ran this establishment for many years. In 1914 a school strike started, lasting for 25 years; the longest strike in history. The school building where the strike occurred is now a museum. Burston has no post office or shop now.

ST. GEORGE'S CHURCH SHIMPLING

SHIMPLING CHURCH, c. 1910

Shimpling Church, dedicated to St. George, is a small building constructed of flint and freestone. It consists of a chancel, nave, north porch and west-facing Norman tower with a round base containing four bells. The spire was added in 1863 and the porch rebuilt around 1900. The people in this picture had just been decorating the church with flowers for a Sunday service. In 1910 Rev. Jeffery Watson Millard was the rector, having held the position since 1854. In 1987 the church was thoroughly restored to a high standard retaining all its charm.

SHIMPLING PLACE FARM, 1911

This photograph was taken at Shimpling Place Farm showing a pond being dug for Mr. Ernest Stearn who farmed Place Farm at the time. All the men in this picture were experienced horsemen working on village farms. The youngest man shown, eighteen-year-old George Mullenger (fourth from the left) worked all his life as a horseman, died recently at the grand age of 98. The rest of the men are: Jimmy Filpby, Peter Seaman, Harry Seaman, Dick Philpot, Fred Filpby, Tom Mullenger and John Dye. The man in the right background is unknown. The population of Shimpling was 157 in 1911.

GISSING BOARD SCHOOL, c. 1925

Gissing Board School was built in 1876 at a cost of £1,120, with accommodation for 88 children and with an average attendance of 60. A Miss Mary England was headmistress and Miss Hilda Scott was the infants mistress. The school closed in 1977, the pupils being transferred to Burston County Primary School. The Gissing school is now used as a village hall. In 1911 the population of the village was about 364.

Gissing Mill.

93423

GISSING MILL, c. 1915

Gissing once had a post windmill adjoining Mill Common at the end of Rectory Road. A Mr. Whitaker Harris was the miller in 1915. He was also the Clerk to the Parish Council. The windmill shown above was badly damaged during a gale many years ago. It was later demolished as it was unsafe and today only the mill house remains.

FRENZE CHURCH, c. 1910

St. Andrew's Church, Frenze is situated in beautiful surroundings in a secluded spot surrounded by woods in what was once the park attached to the old hall. It is a very small building, 70ft by 20ft, consisting only of nave, south porch and poor wooden western bell-cote containing one bell weighing 75lbs. The roof was renewed in 1900. Frenze had a population of 49 in 1911.

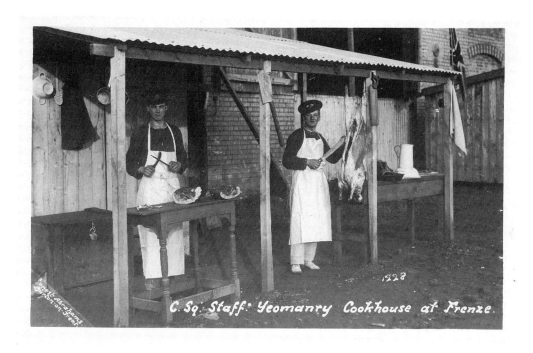

C. Sq. Staff: Yeomanry Cookhouse at Frenze.

FRENZE HALL, c. 1914

This photograph was taken at Frenze Hall in one of the farm buildings which served as a cookhouse during the first world war. Troops of the South Staffordshire Yeomanry were all stationed in the surrounding countryside around Scole and Oakley Park. Ernest Abraham of Burton-on-Trent travelled with the troops to take photographs for making postcards.

DICKLEBURGH RECTORY, p.u. 1910

Dickleburgh Rectory was built in 1839 and situated at the Rushall end of Rectory Road nearly a mile from All Saints Church. The rector in 1910 was the Rev. John Gregory Forbes, M.A. The house and garden were demolished in the 1970s, and a large housing estate built shortly afterwards.

MAIN STREET, DICKLEBURGH, c. 1905

Looking in a southerly direction towards Scole in Main Street. The twice daily horse-drawn mail cart from Scole has just arrived and transferred the mail to the local postman, who has a donkey and small cart on which to make his rounds at 7 a.m. and 2.15 p.m. The post office was run by a John Elliott who was also a grocer and draper. The population of the village was 790 in 1905. The post office was closed in 1970 and demolished to allow the road to be widened. The village sign and a shelter stand on this site today.

DICKLEBURGH, c. 1915

Looking north towards Norwich and showing a view which has changed considerably after 75 years. A bus depot occupies the left-hand side of the road and modern bungalows have been built on the right.

DICKLEBURGH, 26th August, 1912

The heavy and continuous rainfall over two days in late August 1912 caused very extensive damage and flooding throughout many areas of Norfolk. Many riverbanks burst, flooding fields, streets and houses. This view was taken looking west
towards the Burston Road from the main street.

10,588 The Old Sign, Scole Inn.

SCOLE INN

Scole Inn, formerly called The White Hart, was built in 1665 by James Peck; a fine old Jacobean building retaining unique examples of unspoilt architecture and furnishings. This postcard published in 1905 from an early print shows the famous inn sign, an arch of wood extending across the width of the road and carved in oak by a craftsman called Fairchild at a cost of £1,057 – the sign was taken down in 1783. Scole Inn received a daily four-horse mail coach which brought all the mail to the area before the railways arrived. Passenger coaches also called here; the fare from Scole to London was 15/- (75p) outside, and 30/- (£1.50) inside.

GERMAN PRISONERS AT SCOLE, 1914

This photograph was taken outside the Scole Inn. Inside the lorry were German prisoners of war – the first to arrive on 19th October, 1914 – guarded by the South Staffordshire Yeomanry who were stationed in the area. Prisoners were billeted in Billingford maltings at night and during the day put to work cleaning out the River Waveney.

SCOLE SCHOOL, p.u. 1910

A National School was erected in 1853 at a cost of £250 by subscription, and enlarged in 1875 to accommodate 160 children, at a cost of £300. In 1910 the headmaster was a Richard William Clarke who was first appointed in 1884. Children came to the school from beyond the bounds of the parish – they were mainly from Oakley, Stuston, Billingford and Frenze. Notice the variety of hats and caps worn by the children.

SCOLE, c. 1912

Photographed at the junction of the Bungay and the Norwich to Ipswich Roads and showing St. Edmunds House before it was enlarged. This view has changed beyond recognition today with the road and junction having been widened and both sides of the road are lined wth houses. Scole had a population of 519 in 1911.

BAKERY FIRE, SCOLE, 1912

Scole Bakery owned by a Mr. Joseph Powley since 1883 and situated on the corner of the "terrace" opposite Bungay Road, was badly damaged by fire in 1912. The postcard shows the aftermath of the fire, the fire brigade having saved what they could. The bakery was rebuilt before the beginning of the first world war, the business benefitting from the proximity of the North Midland Mounted Brigade who were stationed nearby. Mr. & Mrs. Powley with the help of two assistants, also cooked meats and puddings for the N.C.O.s stationed in the district. Mr. Powley died in 1926 and the business was taken over by John Draper, the baker at Dickleburgh. In 1935 the bakery closed and was converted into a bungalow.

THE FORGE, SCOLE, August 1914

The Forge stood at the top of the hill on the ground adjoining the churchyard. In 1914, the blacksmith was Robert Reeve who had taken over the business following the death of his step-father John Woodcock. While the Mounted Brigade were stationed in the district he worked for the Army, with three army farriers to assist him. Robert Reeve retired in 1944, and the forge was demolished in 1950; the site and the adjacent ground used for the building of three bungalows.

THE CROSS KEYS, SHELFANGER, c. 1925

Photographed outside the Cross Keys public house and showing Mr. Robert Briggs, landlord, and Deafy Brighton's baker's cart which had just made a bread delivery. The public house stood by the main Diss to Attleborough road. It has been closed for many years and the site is now occupied by a garage.

SHELFANGER, p.u. 1914

A delightful view of the village green. On the extreme right, the blacksmith's shop was owned by Mr. Fred Herrell who was also the proprietor of The Crown public house, situated just beyond the village shop which was run by a Mr. John Kerridge. All of these businesses have now closed and the premises converted into private houses. Shelfanger had a populaton of 360 in 1911.

THE OLD OAK INN, WINFARTHING, p.u. 1924

The Old Oak Inn was situated on the outskirts of Winfarthing along the Attleborough Road. Robert Rout was the landlord in 1924. The beautiful thatched inn, full of charm and no doubt many stories to tell, has now closed. In 1911 the population of the village was about 397.

WINFARTHING CHURCH, 1912

Winfarthing Church, dedicated to St. Mary the Virgin, is a plain structure of flint and freestone, consisting of a Decorated chancel, Perpendicular nave, south aisle, north porch and embattled Victorian tower containing six bells, which were recast at the same time the tower and east gable of the nave were restored in 1912, as the photograph shows. Notice the wooden scaffold poles being used lashed together with rope. The rector at this time was Rev. Arthur Edward Church, M.A., who lived in the rectory across the road from the church.

WINFARTHING. 734.

Moling

THE QUEENS HEAD, WORTHAM, 1918

A group of villagers photographed celebrating the announcement of the ending of the first world war and the safe return of soldiers to the village after joining up at the start and during the War. The Queens Head public house was situated on the Bury St. Edmunds road as one enters Wortham from Palgrave and Diss. The landlord at the time was a Mr. Arthur Groom. It has been closed for several years and is now a private house. In 1911 there were around 830 people living in Wortham.

WORTHAM, c. 1908

Wortham, formerly Wortham-Everard and Wortham-Jarvis, is a widely scattered village and parish consisting of 5 hamlets; Long Green, The Ling, Magpie Green, The Marsh and The Brock, situated on the River Waveney which separates this county from Norfolk. This postcard shows the steam-roller mills on the Ling, formerly a windmill converted over to steam after a fire just before the turn of the century. The miller in 1909 was Ernest Youngman. Some buildings remain, along with the miller's house, as a private residence today.

THE POST OFFICE, STUSTON, p.u. 1910

The post office at Stuston stood opposite the village green adjoining the old Bury road. Mr Frederick Elsey was the post-master, taking deliveries from Scole at 7 a.m. daily. He also ran a coach-building business from the adjoining buildings. The population of the village at that time was 179.

THE RECTORY, THRANDESTON, c. 1915

The rector in 1915 was the Rev. William Henry Denison. Notice the splendid Victorian conservatory; a feature which is enjoying a popular revival today. One wonders why such a small village should have had such a large rectory. The building is now a private home. Thrandeston once had a school, post office, a blacksmith, public house and a shop – now there is only a church left in the village. The population in 1911 was around 293.

THE GREEN, PALGRAVE, c. 1910

Photographed close to St. Peter's Church and showing Palgrave Green; the smaller of two greens in the village. The house on the right was formerly a Guildhall, converted into three houses. Adjoining it was The Swan public house, now closed, and today a private house.

PALGRAVE GREEN, p.u. 1912

The Post Office in this picture was situated on the edge of the largest of the two greens in Palgrave. A Mr. George Charles Ford was the postmaster, also a builder and the Parish Clerk. Mail arrived from Diss twice daily at 6.25 a.m. and 1.35 p.m. This post office was transferred to a house on the other side of the green a few years later. The population in the village in 1911 was around 709.

PALGRAVE SCHOOL, c. 1930

The National School was erected in 1853 by the Rev. Charles Martyn, then rector, which included a master's house, and enlarged in 1887 and again in 1894 for 140 children; average attendance 130. The headmaster in 1930 was a Mr. Henry Ford.

W. Baldwin, Dealer in Horses, Palgrave-Diss, Exporter of Worn out Horses to the Continent.

W. BALDWIN , HORSE DEALER, PALGRAVE, p.u. 1908

William Baldwin, horse dealer, photographed at Holly Farm with three horses, worn out or lame, which had just been bought from farms in the district. Mr. Baldwin exported most of the horses to the Continent for their meat.

PALGRAVE 'STARS', 1909–10

Palgrave 'Stars' played in the South Norfolk League in 1909–10 and ended the season as champions of the league. They played on a pitch at the rear of The Priory gardens. This photograph shows the team, supporters and the cup with which they had just been presented. *Back row (left to right):* C.H. Corbett, E. Read, H. Ruffles, Rev. E.L. Savory, W. Haystead, F. Jackson, W.F. Coleman, H. Derisley, J.O. Hinchley, E. Cotton. *Middle row:* H. Thomas, R. Licence, P. Derisley, C. Baldwin (Capt.), W. Mills (Sec.), P. Ward, W. Clarke. *Front row:* C. Tonge, W. Green.

The Supply Stores, Mellis, 1142

THE SUPPLY STORES, MELLIS, p.u. 1910

The Supply Stores stood on Rectory Road. Benjamin Marsh, the proprietor, is shown above standing outside his shop with his wife and children. There was a population of 463 in Mellis in 1910. Sadly, there is no shop or post office in the village today.

THE RAILWAY HOTEL, MELLIS, p.u. 1905

The Railway Hotel is situated on the edge of a very large common at Mellis. Many railway hotels or taverns were built with the coming of the railways in 1849. People travelling long distances in horse-drawn carriages needed accommodation and refreshments. Shortly before a train arrived, a bell would ring in the hotel bar alerting would be passengers of the train's arrival. A Mr. James Manning was the proprietor here in 1905.

THE RAILWAY STATION, MELLIS, p.u. 1912

Mellis Railway Station was opened by the Eastern Union Railway on 2nd July, 1849 for rail services to London. Looking north towards Diss, the postcard shows a train just arrived from Norwich, and on the right, the beginning of a three-mile branch line to Eye which opened on 1st April, 1867. Coal, corn, seed and sugar beet in vast quantities, were handled here by Robinson Bros. and Saville & Co. Ltd., freight sidings and buildings situated on both sides of the main line. Passenger services ceased on the Eye branch line in February 1931 and freight services lasted until 28th July, 1964. Mellis Station closed for passenger and freight services on 5th November, 1966. All station buildings and platform are now demolished, fast electric express trains pass this site now at 100 m.p.h. and modern houses are planned to occupy the station site.

COMIC POSTCARD, p.u. 1904

A mass-produced comic postcard from the 'Premier' Series, known as a stock card, and overprinted to order for any location nationwide.